COUNTING BY

FIVES

Kay Robertson

rourkeeducationalmedia.com

*Scan for Related Titles
and Teacher Resources*

Teaching Focus:
Alliteration- Have students find words with the same beginning sounds.

Before Reading:

Building Academic Vocabulary and Background Knowledge
Before reading a book, it is important to set the stage for your child or student by using pre-reading strategies. This will help them develop their vocabulary, increase their reading comprehension, and make connections across the curriculum.

1. Read the title and look at the cover. *Let's make predictions about what this book will be about.*
2. Take a picture walk by talking about the pictures/photographs in the book. Implant the vocabulary as you take the picture walk. Be sure to talk about the text features such as headings, Table of Contents, glossary, bolded words, captions, charts/diagrams, or Index.
3. Have students read the first page of text with you then have students read the remaining text.
4. Strategy Talk – use to assist students while reading.
   - Get your mouth ready
   - Look at the picture
   - Think…does it make sense
   - Think…does it look right
   - Think…does it sound right
   - Chunk it – by looking for a part you know
5. Read it again.
6. After reading the book complete the activities below.

High Frequency Words
Flip through the book and locate how many times the high frequency words were used.

after
came
count
fives
me
then

After Reading:

Comprehension and Extension Activity
After reading the book, work on the following questions with your child or students in order to check their level of reading comprehension and content mastery.

1. *What was happening to the child in the book? What happened at the end of the book?* (Summarize)
2. *What is different about the animals used in the beginning of the book through the end of the book? Why?* (Inferring)
3. *Which animal in the book is the scariest one? Why?* (Text to self connection)
4. *What pattern do you notice when you count by fives?* (Asking questions)

Extension Activity
Counting by fives really matters! We count by fives when we use nickels. Each nickel is worth 5 cents. You count nickels the same as you count by fives. Try it out! Use play coins or real nickels to practice counting by fives. Take three nickels. How much are three nickels worth? How many nickels do you need to make 100? Did you know 20 nickels equals a dollar? How many dollars would 40 nickels equal?

I went to bed and what did I see? All kinds of critters chasing after me. Oh my! Let's count these critters by fives.

First came five enormous elephants stomping after me.

ROARRRRRR!

5

Then came ten roaring bears chasing after me.

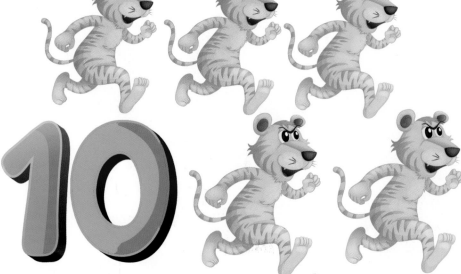

5

10

Then came fifteen terrible tigers chasing after me.

GRRRRRR

Then came twenty frightening fish swimming after me.

5

10

15

Then came twenty-five chattering monkeys swinging after me.

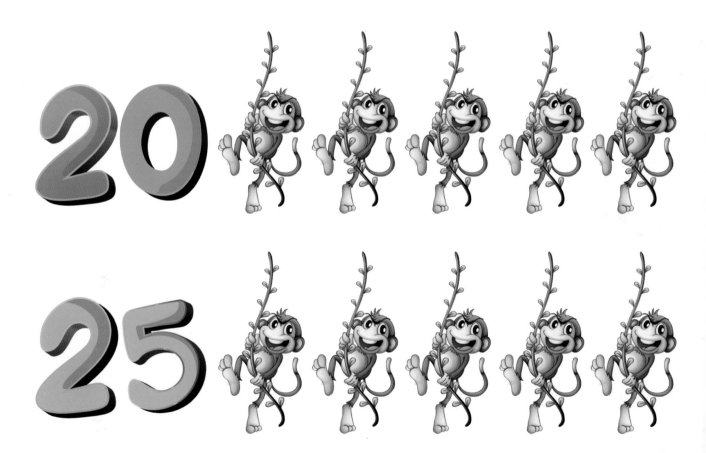

5

Ssssssss
Ssssssss

10

Ssssssss
Ssssssss

15

Ssssssss
Ssssssss

20

Ssssssss
Ssssssss

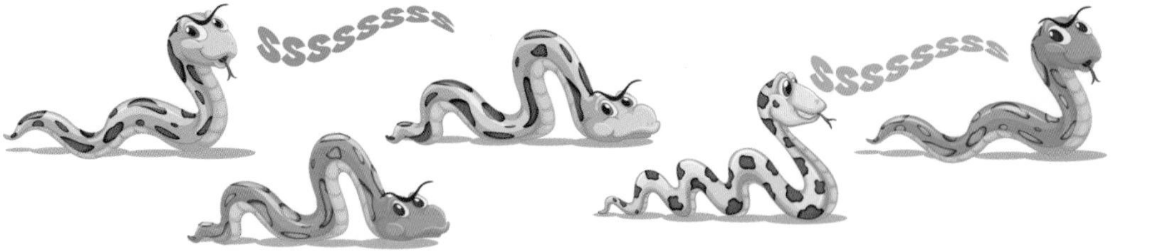

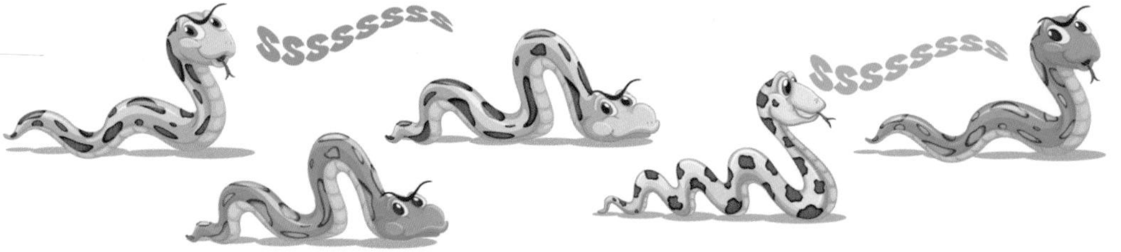

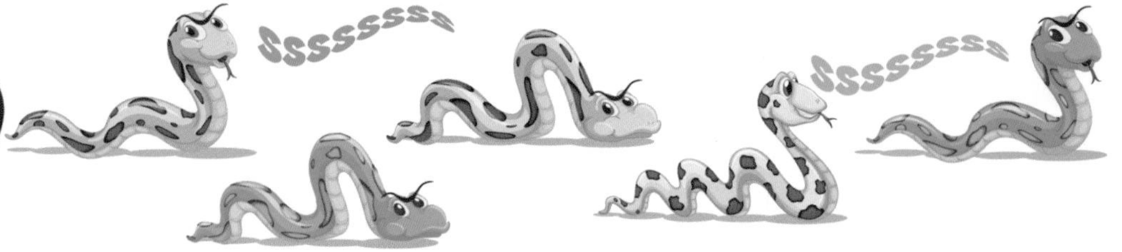

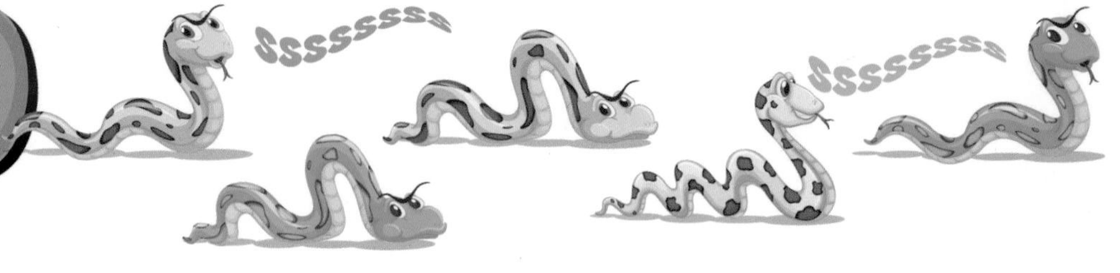

Then came thirty hissing snakes slithering after me.

Then came thirty-five big, black bats swooping after me.

EEK!

25

30

35

EEK!

Then came forty hairy, scary spiders crawling after me.

Then came forty-five buzzing bees zooming after me.

buzzzzzzz

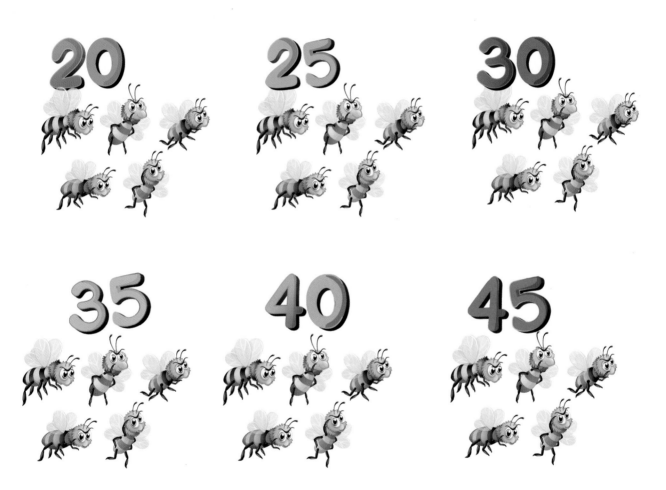

20 25 30
35 40 45

Then came fifty angry ants marching after me.

And I said, "That's enough counting by fives. Time to wake-up!"

23

Index

Websites

http://pbskids.org/games/123/

http://www.primarygames.com/math/
   fishycount/

http://www.ixl.com/math/kindergarten/
   represent-numbers-up-to-20

Meet The Author!
www.meetREMauthors.com

About the Author

Living in Florida, Kay Robertson is used to bumping into many different critters every day. But the hissing, slithering critters that she finds in her yard still give her quite a fright!

www.rourkeeducationalmedia.com

PHOTO/ILLUSTRATION CREDITS: Cover, Illustrated numbers and animals throughout © Matthew Cole/shutterstock; page 3 and page 23 photos © Deyan Georgiev/shutterstock; bubbles page 10 and 11 © Nickylarson974

Edited by: Luana Mitten

Cover design and Interior design: by Nicola Stratford
www.nicolastratford.com

Library of Congress PCN Data

Counting by Fives / Kay Robertson
(Concepts)
ISBN 978-1-63430-054-4 (hard cover)
ISBN 978-1-63430-084-1 (soft cover)
ISBN 978-1-63430-112-1 (e-Book)
Library of Congress Control Number: 2014953332

Rourke Educational Media
Printed in the United States of America, North Mankato, Minnesota

Also Available as: